adult content
contains profanity

offensive

1. ADJECTIVE

Something that is offensive upsets or embarrasses people because it is rude or insulting

If you are easily offended yet you continue to read from this point you have forfeited the right to complain.

In all seriousness, it is almost impossible to find online memes that do not contain the odd profanity. No one is asking you to chant them out loud; if something here offends, just pull up your big-boy/girl pants, take a deep breath and step over it!

If you are still with me, enjoy!   ;-)

♦♦♦♦

2019 ends quietly with stories of a little known virus in some far-off land.

Early 2020 and Covid-19, Coronavirus (or *the Rona/Boomer Remover*) arrives with a vengeance and the shit really hits the fan worldwide!

Cue the great toilet paper, PPE and hand sanitizer stampedes of March 2020 unleashing an avalanche of sometimes dark but hilarious memes...

> **MIDNIGHT DECEMBER 31ST 2019**
>
> I CAN'T BELIEVE WE STAYED UP AND SCREAMED HAPPY NEW YEAR FOR THIS BULLSHIT!

I miss the days when you sneezed and people would say a polite "Bless you", now they say "Get the fuck away from me!"

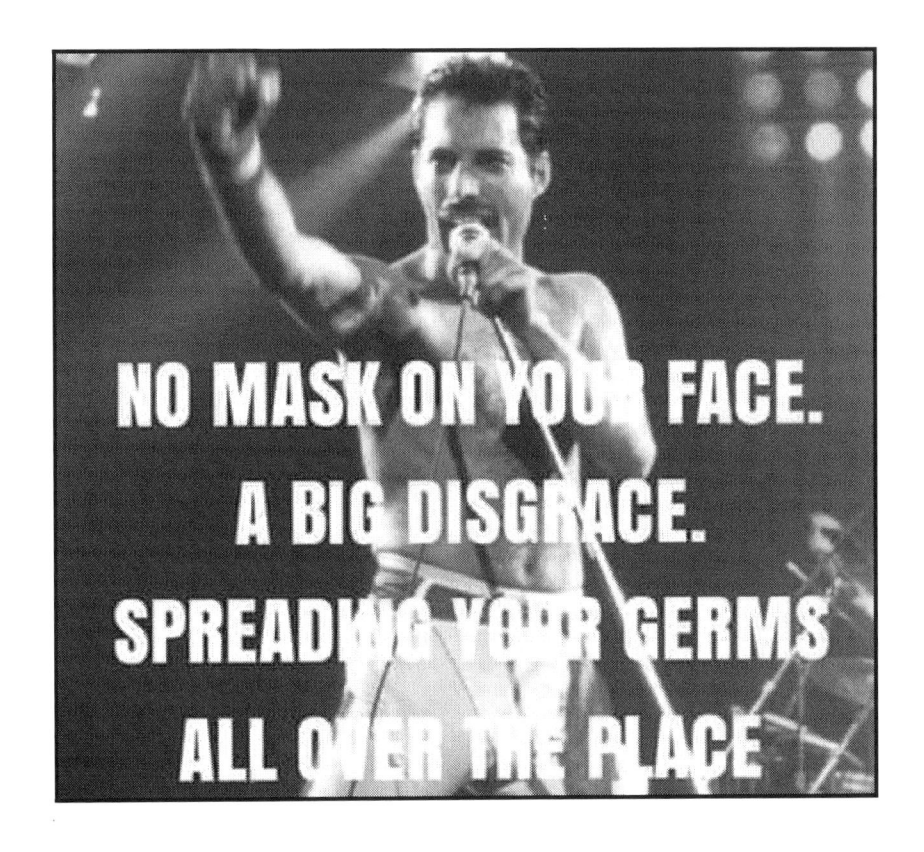

NO MASK ON YOUR FACE.
A BIG DISGRACE.
SPREADING YOUR GERMS
ALL OVER THE PLACE

I have ex's that are waaay more toxic than the Corona Virus...
⚠️😆⚠️
I fear nothing!
🤣🕺🤣

Me every time I feel the slightest tickle in my throat.

"oh Lord, it got me."

practice good high jean

You can say "have a nice day." and no problem. But you can't say "enjoy the next 24 hours!" and not sound vaguely threatening.

This is Bill.
Bill wants to take a trip,
but bill doesnt want to contract corona.

Bill chooses to take a trip at home.
With mushrooms.

Be responsible.
Be like Bill.

I have no clue what's open or closed anymore. I just walk towards automatic doors and if my face hits the glass I turn around and go home.

You can go out...

But, you can't go Out out..

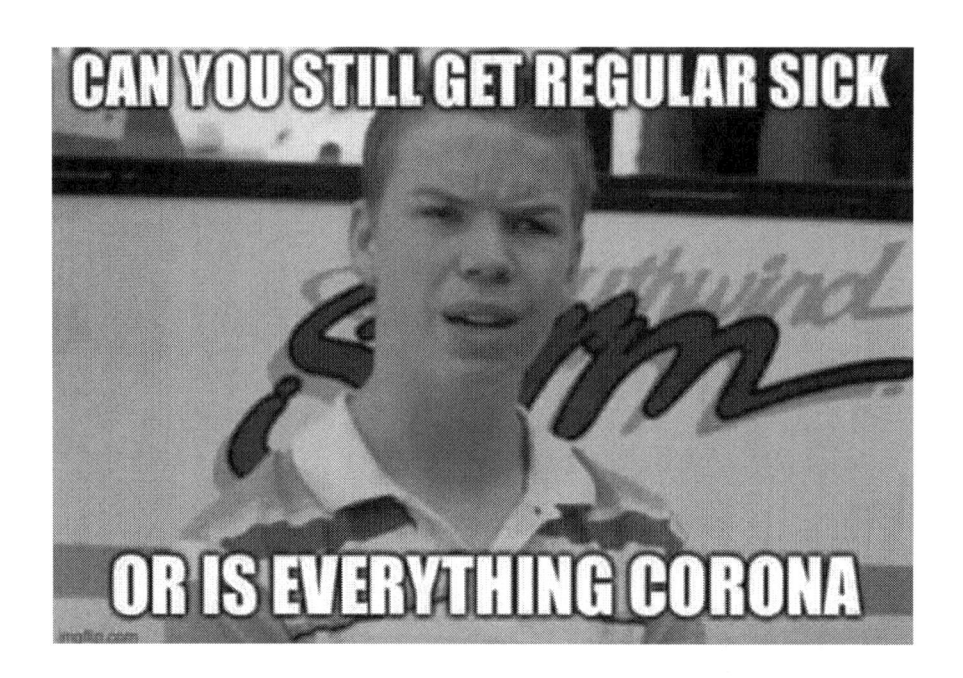

CAN YOU STILL GET REGULAR SICK OR IS EVERYTHING CORONA

Just picked up my social distance support animal.

Some people aren't shaking hands because of the Coronavirus. I'm not shaking hands because everyone's out of toilet paper. #aussieas

I washed my hands so much due to #CODVID19, that my exam notes from 1995 resurfaced

Look me straight in the eye and tell me the truth about Covid-19

The government:

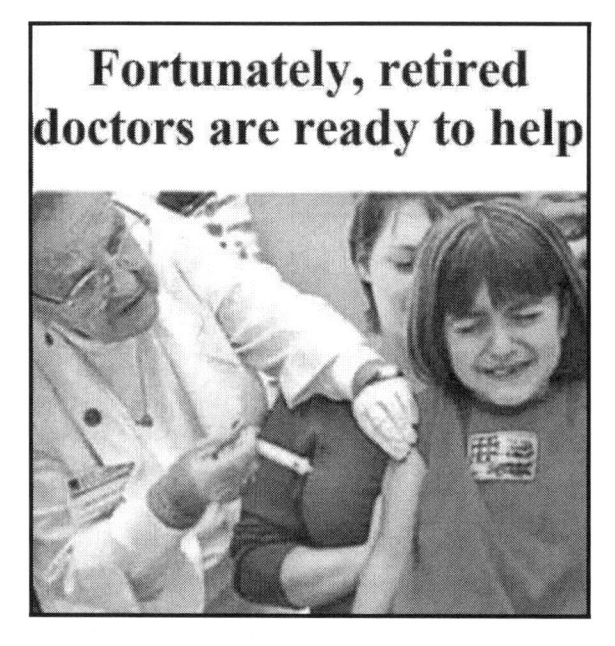

Fortunately, retired doctors are ready to help

AT THIS POINT I'M STUCK BETWEEN IDK, IDC AND IDGAF.

For Your Safety
&
Due to The Carnivorous

We Will Not Be
Able to Open
The Pool This Season.

When I'm at the store and getting something I grab the one behind it because I think there's something wrong with the one in front.

JUST WHEN YOU THOUGHT YOU'VE SEEN IT ALL...

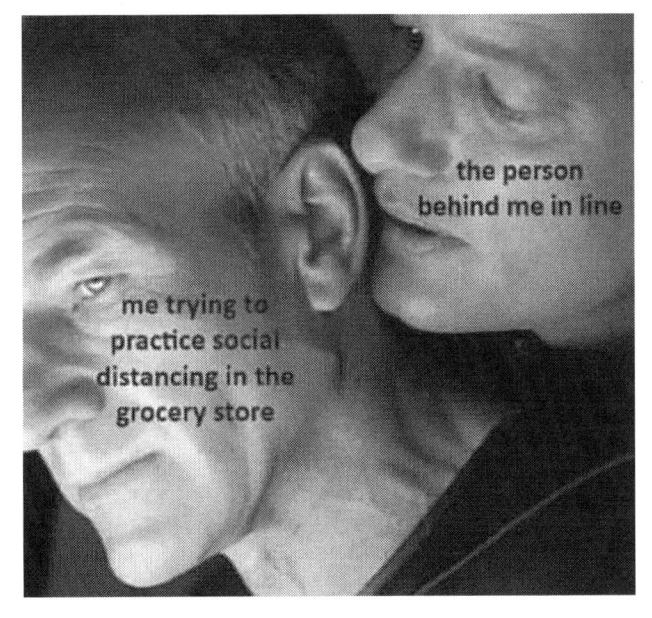

@medcapsus

the person behind me in line

me trying to practice social distancing in the grocery store

ROMANCE NOVELS WRITTEN DURING COVID 19 WILL BE LIKE .... AS SHE SLOWLY SLIPPED HER MASK DOWN AND REMOVED HER GLOVES... 😆😆

YOU ARE GOING TO BE FINE.

YOU COME FROM A STRONG LINE OF LUNATICS.

THIS IS A BUNNY BUTT.

NO VIRUSES. NO POLITICS. JUST A BUNNY BUTT.

ANYONE WANT TO MEET FOR LUNCH

WE CAN ORDER DRIVE THRU AND PULL UP NEXT TO EACH OTHER LIKE THE POLICE DO

Flirting in 2020 be like...

BLINK IF YOU WANT ME.

What did YOU do in the Corona outbreak Dad?

i bought loads of stuff i didnt need

fuckin knob

GOVERNORS: "OUTSIDE IS NOW OPEN"

ME: WAITING TO SEE WHAT HAPPENS TO THE FIRST ROUND OF PEOPLE

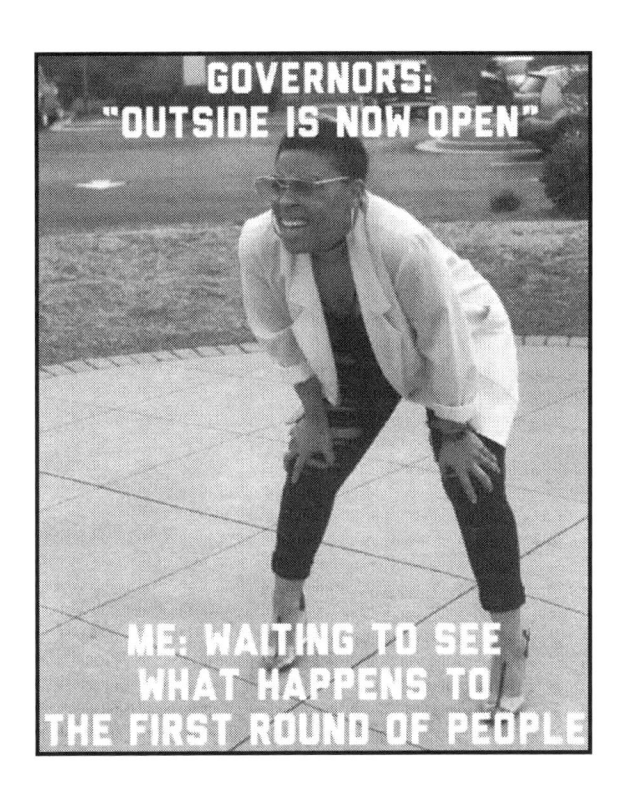

Me coming online with my stolen Memes to cheer you all up..

I'M ESSENTIAL..

I asked my missus to dress up in a nurses uniform last night, she got all excited and asked me what I was going to do to her. I told her I was driving her to the supermarket to get a loaf of bread.

Of all the things I learned in grade school, trying to avoid Cooties was the last one I expected to use.

INHALE

EXHALE

BRIGHT and EARLY Books for BEGINNING Beginners

Things I Will Put Up Your Ass

If You Don't Put On That Fucking Mask

By Dr. Seuss

PEOPLE BORN IN MARCH / APRIL IN THE COMING WEEKS

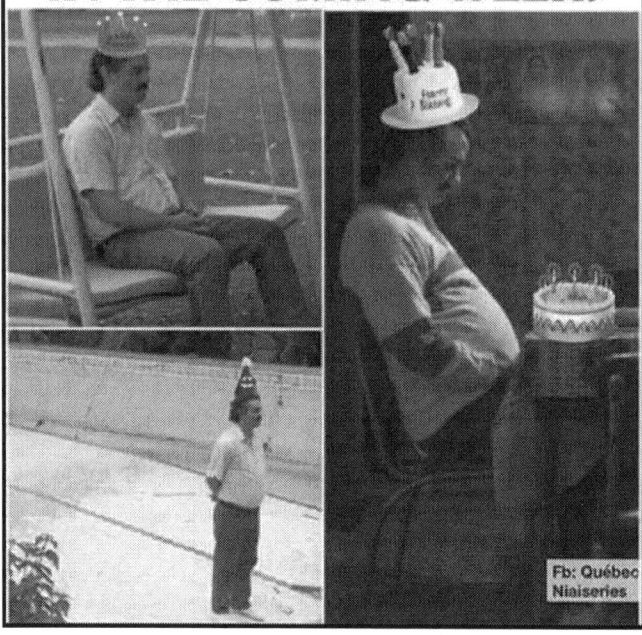

Fb: Québec Niaiseries

Due to the Coronavirus, Bettie White has been placed inside a bank vault protected by Chuck Norris.

"2020 can't get any worse"

April:

I just dumped a pack of M&M's into my mask at work and am slowly eating them like a horse.

I love the pandemic.

Dogs don't get the virus so are free to travel

If the past few weeks have taught us anything, it's that stupidity spreads faster than the virus.

Ash
@cray_at_home_ma

I turned off the TV today and made my kids play board games like it was 1955 and now I know why all of our grandparents were alcoholics

I have a fever

Y'all are doing crafts, starting to make your own Gardens... it's a slippery slope

Alarming Report Suggests Americans Can't Go Much Longer Without Jobs And Haircuts Before Becoming Hippies

"2019 is going to be my year"

Me in April:

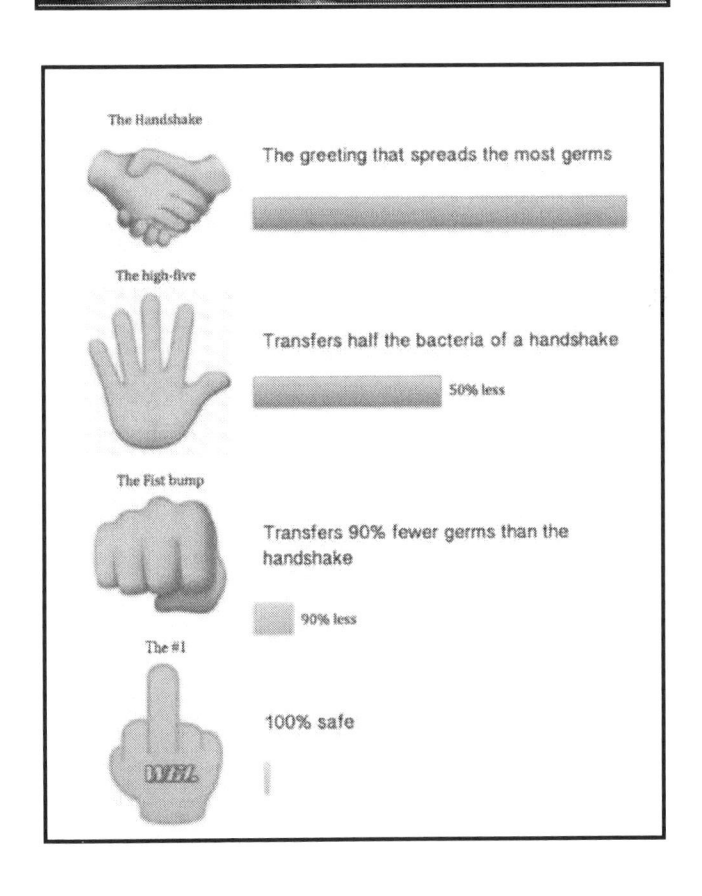

[Image: rear of a double-decker bus with destination sign reading "Help Me"]

The Handshake

The greeting that spreads the most germs

The high-five

Transfers half the bacteria of a handshake

50% less

The Fist bump

Transfers 90% fewer germs than the handshake

90% less

The #1

100% safe

How I'm gonna feel when thrift stores open back up!

How I feel when I take off my mask after work.

CONGRATULATIONS YOU SUCCESSFULLY MADE IT TO THE END OF APRIL!

WELCOME TO LEVEL 5 OF JUMANJI!

FUNNY THOUGHTS AND JOKES

MY TOLERANCE FOR IDIOTS IS EXTREMELY LOW TODAY. I USED TO HAVE SOME IMMUNITY BUILT UP, BUT OBVIOUSLY THERE IS A NEW STRAIN OUT THERE.

When you hate people more than the virus

Health Report: Two-Faced Bitches Still Only Need One Mask

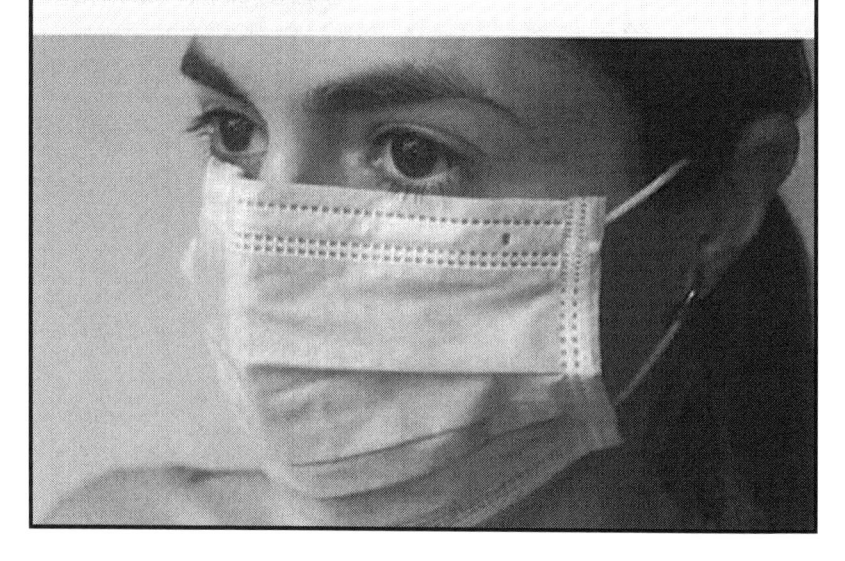

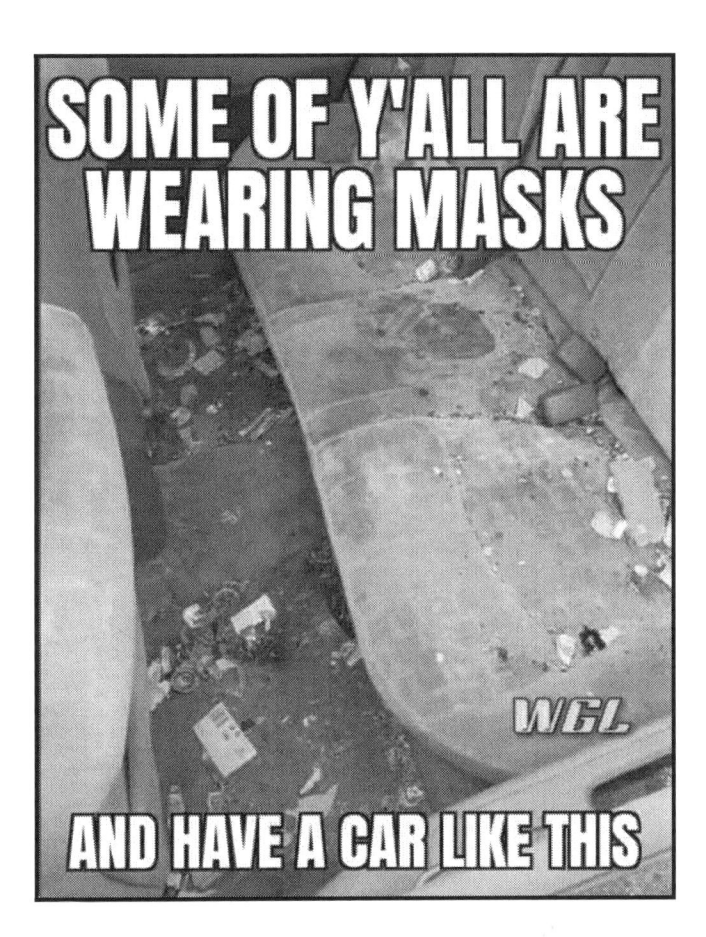

SOME OF Y'ALL ARE WEARING MASKS AND HAVE A CAR LIKE THIS

IF YOU'RE UGLY, BUT HAVE PRETTY EYES...

THIS IS YOUR CHANCE!!!

Wash your hands like you're washing Jason Momoa

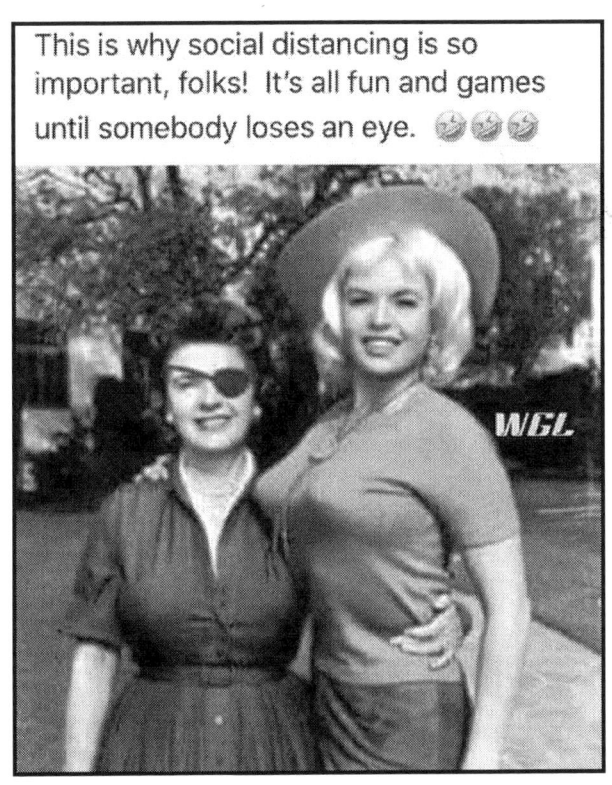

WASHING YOUR HANDS For ≥ 20 seconds is important to HELP STOP THE SPREAD of COVID
YES 20 SECS SEEMS LIKE FOREVER But...
A LOT of MEN THINK 2 Mins is FOREVER TOO 😊

This is why social distancing is so important, folks! It's all fun and games until somebody loses an eye. 🤣🤣🤣

The Hills are closed

Tillie putting on her steel toe ass kickers to help maintain a safe social distance at the grocery store.

SOCIAL DISTANCING WINNER OF THE DAY.

All I'm saying is if we give everybody a hit of acid they won't be bored for 8-12 hours and they won't go outside because of the fucking dragons

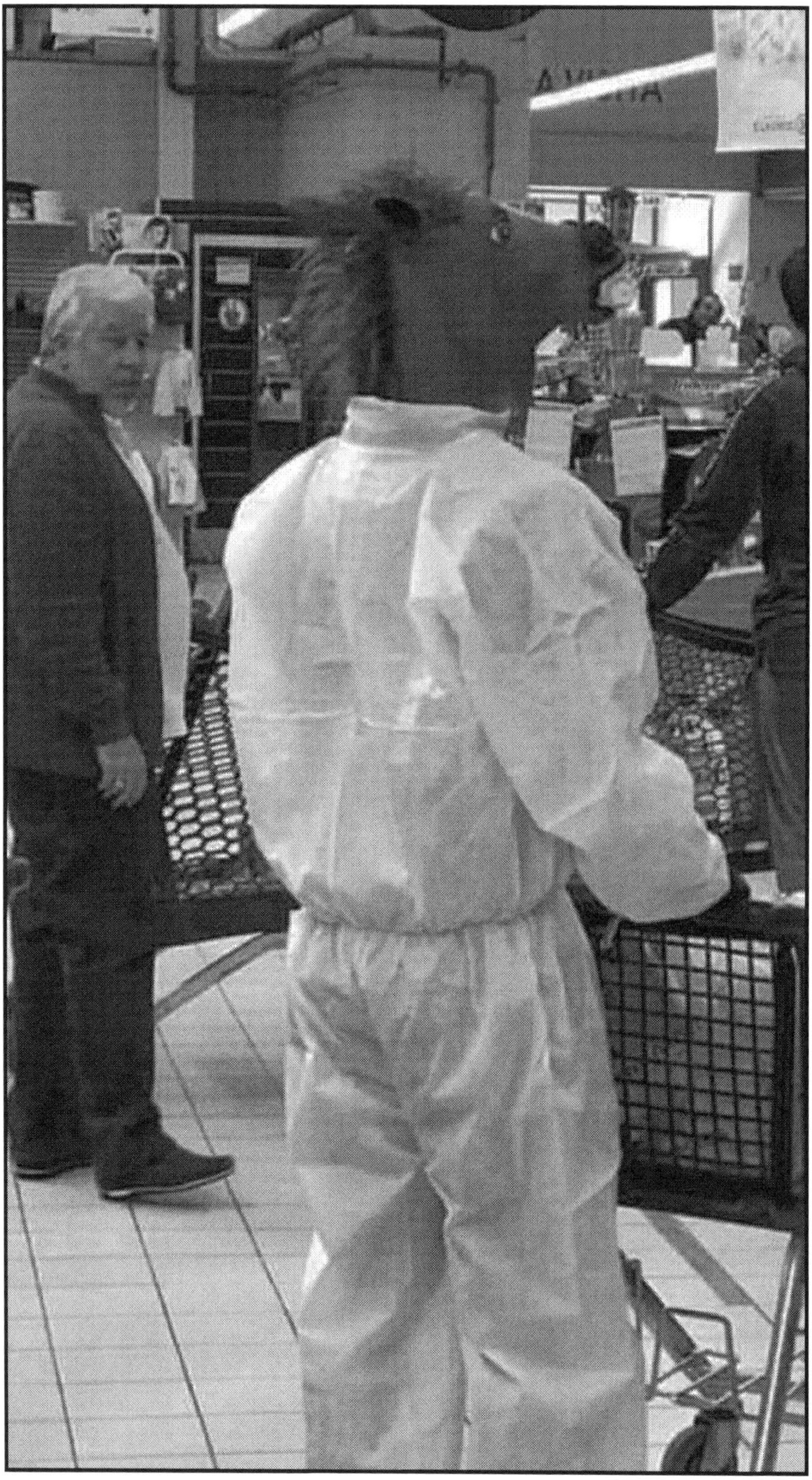

SOME OF Y'ALL GOT SPAGHETTI SAUCE STUCK IN YOUR MICROWAVE SINCE 1996

AND YOU'RE IN A STORE ACTING LIKE A FOOL OVER LYSOL

I miss sh*tting on people!

There's a plant that will protect you against the corona virus

Plant your ass on the couch and don't leave home

WORKING FROM HOME

I love these lazy Saturdays.

It's Wednesday, Homer.

Emily Annette
@EmilyAnnette6

At the grocery. Wearing my mask. Lady behind me, snarky & loud enough to make sure I heard, "don't guess she realizes that stupid mask won't do any good." Me: "Honey, I'm an off duty nurse, I'm wearing it to protect YOU. But, I can take it off if you'd like." She practically ran.

I KNOW
EVERYTHING HAPPENS
FOR A REASON

BUT WHAT THE FUCK

WAIT, SO YOU'RE TELLING ME THAT MY CHANCE OF SURVIVING ALL THIS IS DIRECTLY LINKED TO THE COMMON SENSE OF OTHERS?

"Bitch, did you get fired?!"

JP @jpbrammer · Apr 1
I wonder if our pets are starting to be like ok the fuck is going on...

FUCK

WOODROW PEEL
@WoodyLuvsCoffee

I just Clorox wiped a bottle of Purell and Purelled my hands cuz I touched the Clorox canister.

How far down a rabbit hole does this go?

Whoever threw this away, please pick it up. The weather forecast said it is going to rain and we already have enough going on.

Introverts watching extroverts freaking out

Pathetic.

You must stay in your home ma'am, dick is NOT considered essential

Due to Corona virus we are self-isolating. No one may enter except:

Keanu Reeves
Matthew McConaughey
George Clooney
and those firefighter guys holding puppies who we saw on a calendar.

"Is that hand sanitizer in your pocket or are you just happy to be within six feet of me?"

IF YOU GREW UP IN THE 80's YOU'RE SAFE

THE THIN PERMANENT SHELL COATING OF AQUA NET IS KEEPING YOUR LUNGS PROTECTED

HOME IS WHERE YOUR ASS SHOULD BE

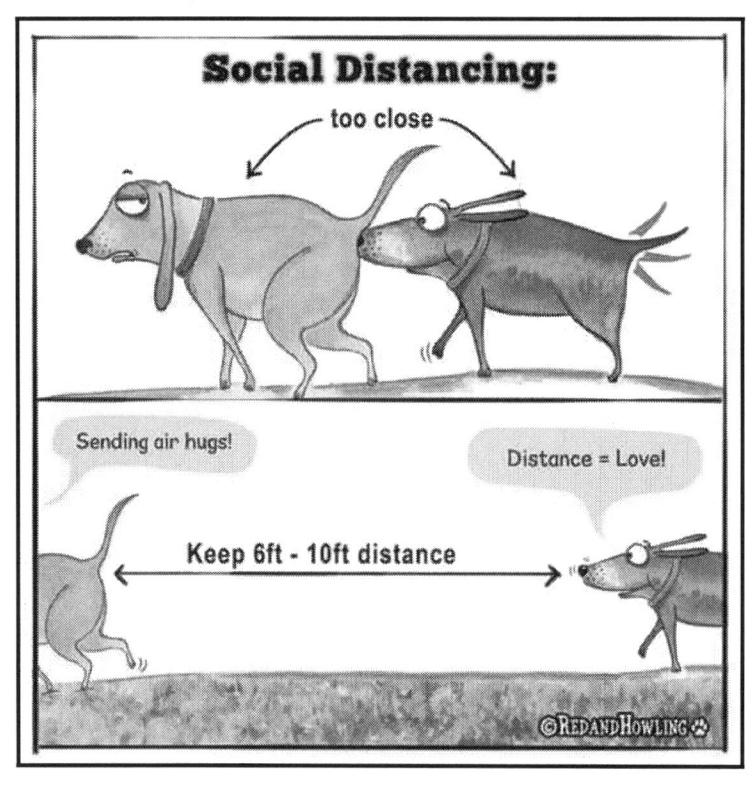

NO, I'M NOT COMING DOWN!
We've been on 20 walks today. Leave me alone.

Social Distancing:

too close

Sending air hugs!

Distance = Love!

Keep 6ft - 10ft distance

©RedAndHowling

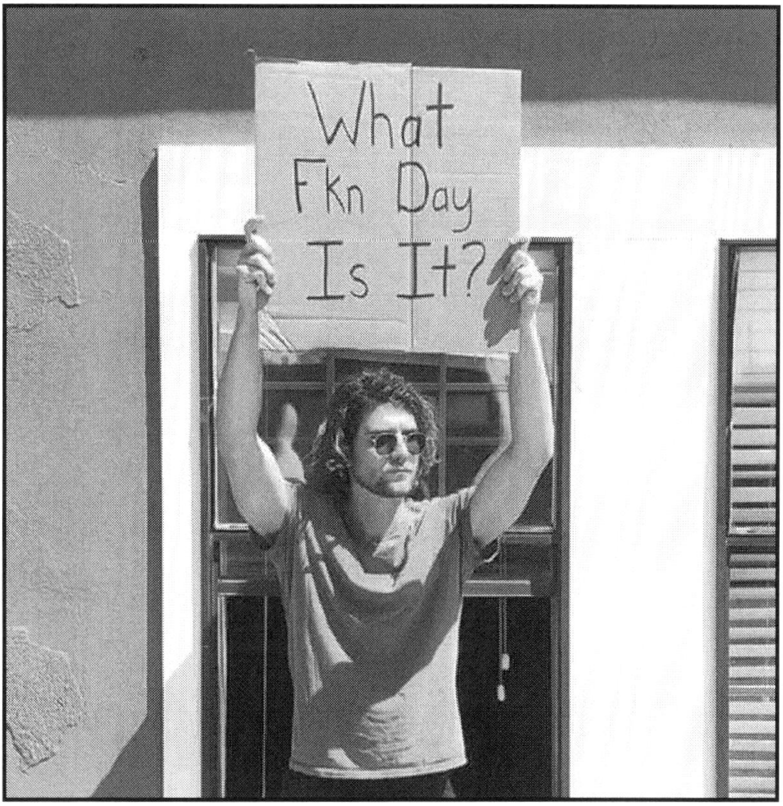
What
Fkn Day
Is It?

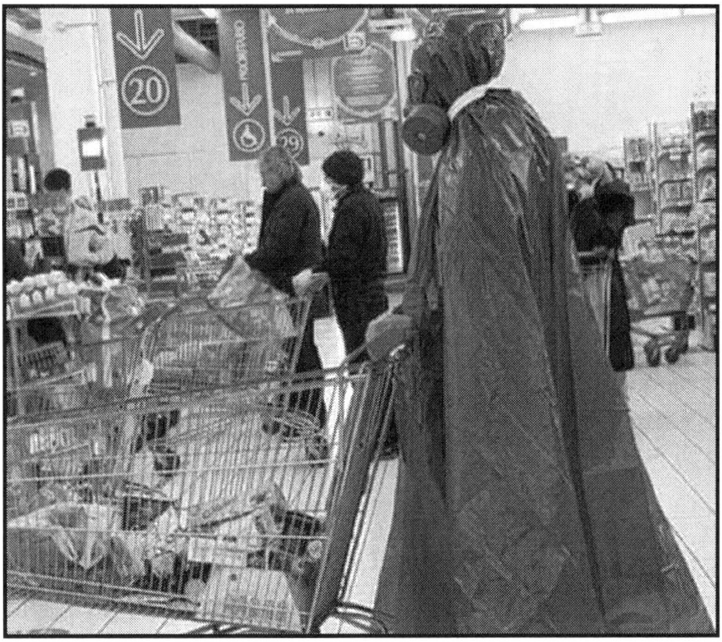
20
29

STAY AWAY FROM ME YOU SICK FUCKERS WHO SHOULD HAVE STAYED HOME.
BLUNTCARD

"We need to talk, Karen.
Why are you in my house so much lately?"
Betabrand

CORONAVIRUS SHUTDOWN:
DAY 1: **Day 7**

Let's Disinfect The Fuck out of Everything

The Ladybird 'Under Five' Series

> A meteorite!

> Quick! Lets go get toilet paper!

I want to get quarantined with you.

— flirting in 2020

SOCIAL DISTANCING IS EASY FOR ME

WHEN IS THE LAST TIME Y'ALL SEEN ME IN PERSON?

ALL OF THOSE IN FAVOR OF BITCH SLAPPING STUPID PEOPLE, SAY "I"

The CDC: the best way to fight Covid19 is to wash your hands often with soap and water

The US: panic buys water

The CDC: we said SOAP too

The US: panic buys toilet paper

The CDC:

The people that won't self quarantine are the same assholes that would hide a zombie bite

BREAKING NEWS

PEOPLE ARE FUCKING STUPID

A NEW STUDY REVEALS THAT MOST PEOPLE ARE DUMB AS SHIT

AFTER ALL THE STUPID THINGS I'VE DONE IN MY LIFE

IF I DIE BECAUSE I TOUCHED MY FACE

I'M GONNA BE PISSED

JUST ASKING TO BE BURGLED

DOWN THE PUB

THEY SAY, "DON'T HANG OUT WITH MORE THAN 10 PEOPLE"

SHIT, I DON'T EVEN LIKE 10 PEOPLE !

I never thought "I wouldn't touch him/her with a ten-foot pole" would become national policy, but here we are.

HR explaining to me that I can't be yelling THIS MUTHAFUKA GOT THE RONA at every co-worker who coughs.

TRAVEL PLANS FOR THE WEEKEND:

TO THE WINDOW

TO THE WALL

Me: Why do I have to come into work?

Employer: Because you're Essential..

Me:

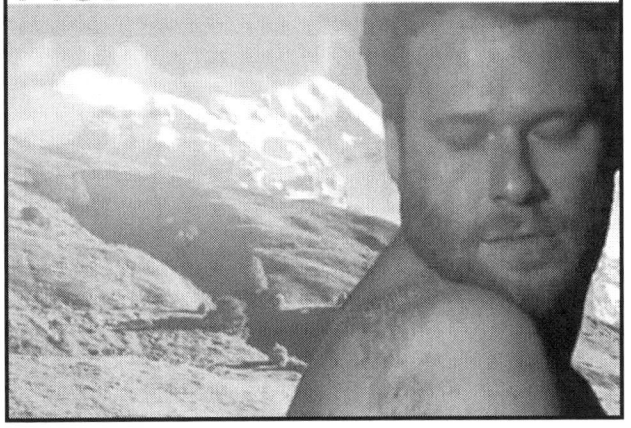

WHAT ARE WE ALL GONNA DIE FROM?!	CORONAVIRUS!
WHAT ARE THE SYMPTOMS?!	FEVER & A COUGH!
WHAT SHOULD WE BUY?!	ALL THE TOILET PAPER!!!!

Gas is 1.89 and I saw three mullets on my way to work, what year is it?

Tupperware Lady 1, Coronavirus 0

I just coughed in a Xbox Live chat and someone said "awe fuck no" and left.

ALL OF A SUDDEN

EVERYBODY HAS BECOME SHELDON

Before you complain about your current situation, just remember, someone is quarantined with your ex.

America sure is having some bad luck. It's almost like it was built on an ancient Indian burial ground.

WHEN YOU'RE UGLY BUT YOU HAVE TOILET PAPER

the richest family in 2020

How I thought I'd look during the apocalypse

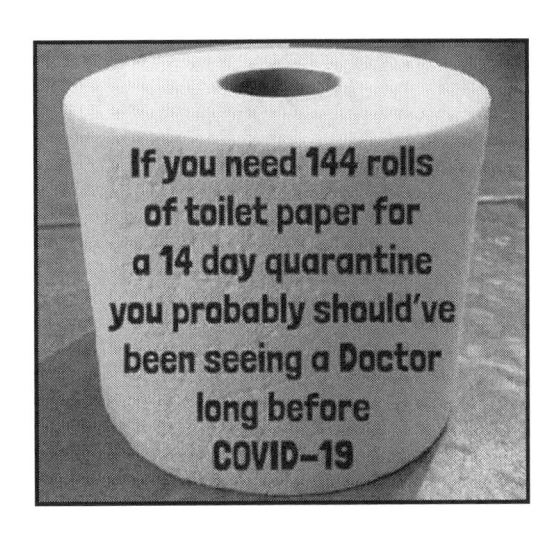

How I really look

If you need 144 rolls of toilet paper for a 14 day quarantine you probably should've been seeing a Doctor long before COVID-19

Hello.

Is It Me You're Looking For?

Due to the short supply of disinfectants and cleaning supplies, dirty deeds will no longer be done dirt cheap

Guess someone told the Amish.
@CincyMeme

We all owe 2019 an apology for what we said about it.

January 1st: "This is my year!"

March 20th: *wiping my ass with a coffee filter*

If I learned anything from movies, I am too out of shape for what is about to happen.

ALL OF US STUCK AT HOME

SHOULD CALL RANDOM NUMBERS IN INDIA AND ASK THEM ABOUT THEIR EXTENDED CAR WARRANTY

WHEN THE FOOD RUNS OUT, WE'LL STILL HAVE EACH OTHER...

Everytime I feel a lil tingle in my throat

Is that you rona

HOW TO PROPERLY GREET SOMEONE DURING THE CORONAVIRUS OUTBREAK

THEY SAID A MASK AND GLOVES WERE ENOUGH TO GO TO THE GROCERY STORE

THEY LIED, EVERYBODY ELSE HAD CLOTHES ON

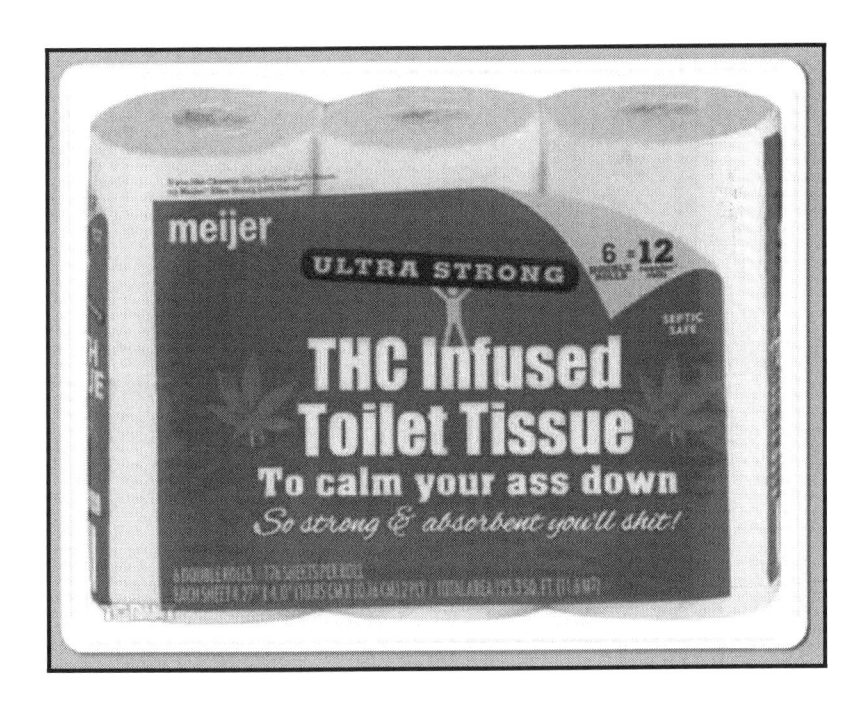

meijer

ULTRA STRONG 6 = 12

THC Infused Toilet Tissue
To calm your ass down
So strong & absorbent you'll shit!

Me: I think I'm ready to date again...

The universe : oh yeah? *releases world-wide virus preventing all human interaction*

Me: well played.

"wish I could be.. part of that world"

bitch no the fuck you dont

YourChildhoodRuined.com

DON'T PET MY EMOTIONAL SUPPORT TOILET PAPER

How to keep from touching your face

Me holding in my coughs in public so ppl don't try and quarantine me 😂

Anyone who is acting like buying hand sanitizer and soap is new, remember who they are and don't eat their cooking

If tomorrow is the start of the apocalypse, do we start with the Mad Max outfits and hairdos immediately, or does that happen later?

THE RETURN LINES ON APRIL 1st. WHEN RENT IS DUE.

Friend: **Worries about toilet paper**

Me: ....

A decision was made

Since everyone has started washing their hands like we're supposed to, we'll be working on shapes and colors for the next few weeks.

JUST THINK, PEOPLE WHO KISS THEIR DOGS AND CATS KNOWING THEY LICK THEIR ASSES AND BALLS, ARE THE ONES IN A PANIC TO BUY A HAND SANITIZER.

Dating ain't just dating anymore...ur picking ur potential apocalypse partner so choose wisely folks

CDC says to avoid Coronavirus, stay home, avoid physical contact and stay away from crowds.

Bitch, I've been training for this moment my whole life.

TODAY IS BROUGHT TO YOU BY THE LETTER C AND THE NUMBER 19

SORRY FOLKS

THE WORLD IS CLOSED

WHEN YOUR COWORKER

COUGHS

Ria Lina ✅
@rialina_

Since we are not to shake hands anymore I propose we curtesy and bow as they did in the times of Jane Austen.

Gender is irrelevant, whosoever bows first, the other must curtesy in return.

Let the greetings begin.

Therapist: you can't just lock people out of your life

Me:

Everybody talking about washing your hands. Some of y'all need to hit that butt crack while you're at it...

Boss: To prevent spreading germs in the workplace, can anyone think of any good alternatives to handshakes to greet people at work?

Me:

> God bless the hundreds of people doomsday prepping at Costco right now and still eating the little food samples sitting out for everyone to touch #coronavirus

Mike is Happy (relatively)
@mikeishappy

Forget #Coronavirus, the human race is much more likely to be wiped out by the Kentucky Fried Donut Sandwich.

> STAY TOGETHER OR YOU'LL END UP AS TOILET PAPER

FIELD TRIP TODAY!

NEIL DIAMOND: hands
CDC: yes, wash them for at least 20 seconds
NEIL DIAMOND: touching hands
CDC: no, please don't touch hands
NEIL DIAMOND: reaching out
CDC: avoiding that too
NEIL DIAMOND: touching me
CDC: oh hell
NEIL DIAMOND: TOUCHING YOU

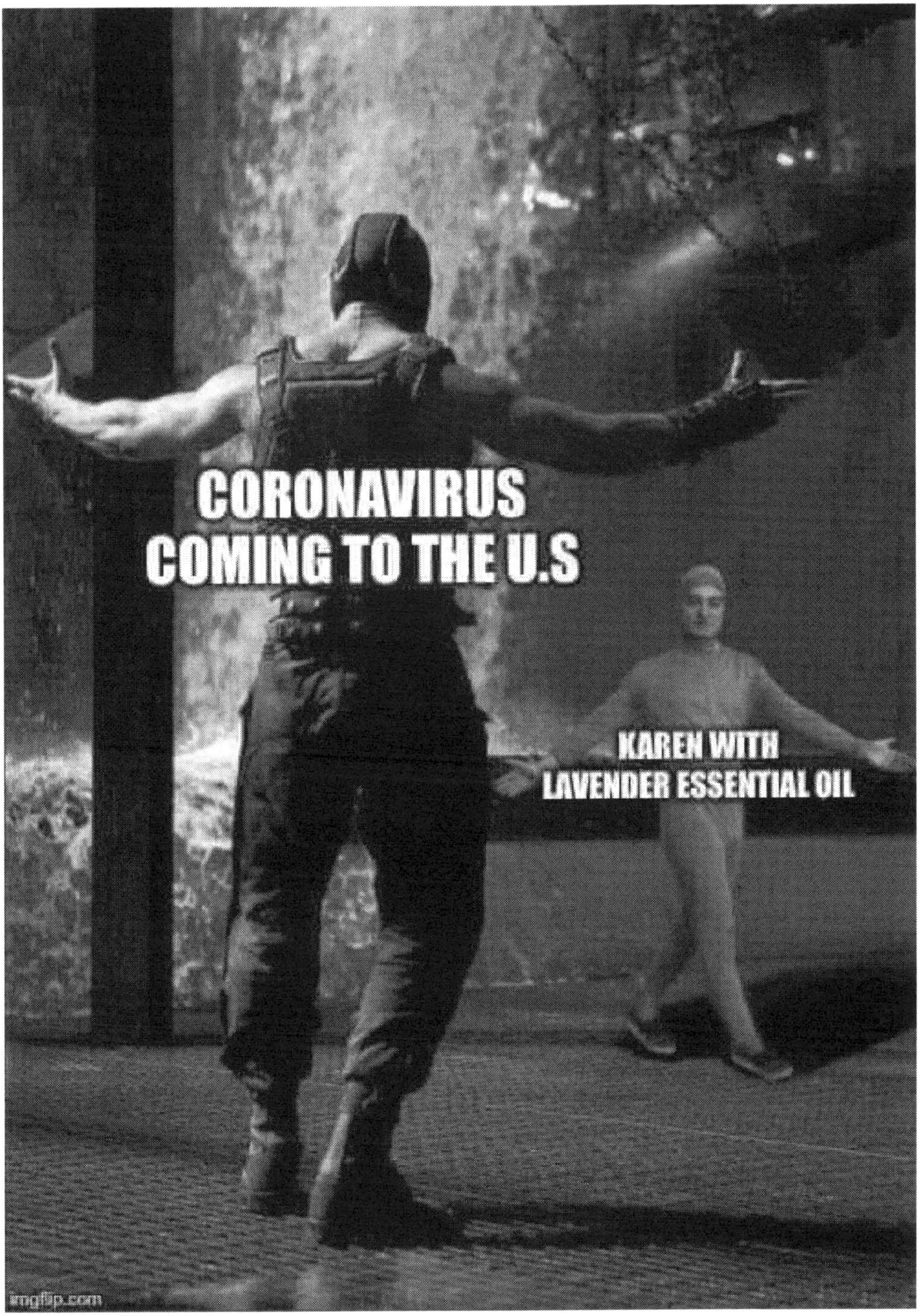
CORONAVIRUS
COMING TO THE U.S
KAREN WITH
LAVENDER ESSENTIAL OIL
imgflip.com

> Who ever drank MD20/20 and smoked mexican brick weed out of a soda can as a teenager are immune to Coronavirus.

Corona ✓
@corona

Again, you don't get the coronavirus by drinking our beer! Coronavirus symptoms include fever, runny nose and coughing. Symptoms of drinking Corona include gagging, craving Taco Bell and waking up next to someone you wish you wouldn't have.

27/01/2020, 01:46 PM

2K RETWEETS **312K** LIKES

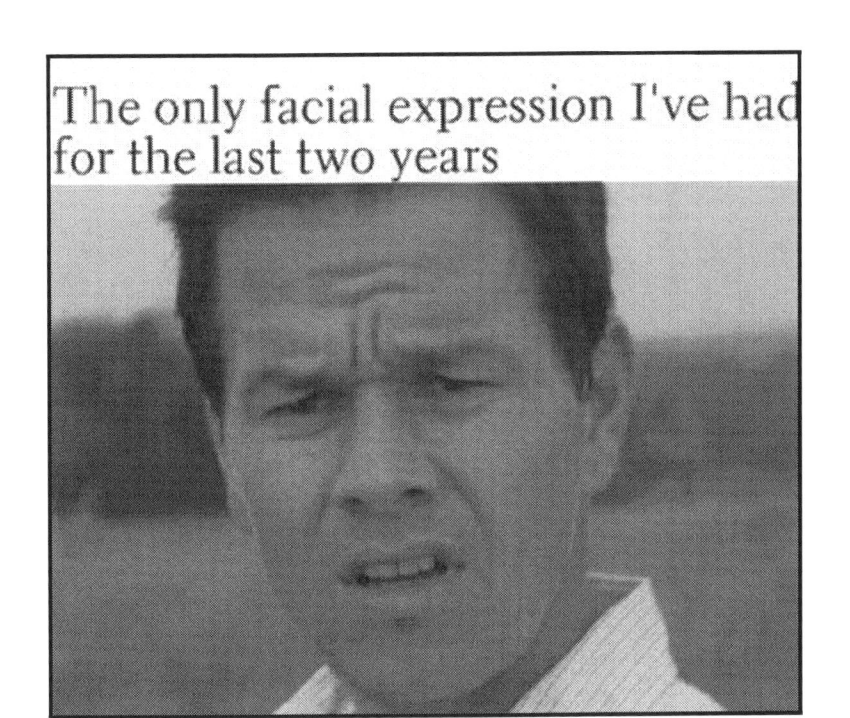

The only facial expression I've had for the last two years

psst... I got toilet paper... the two ply stuff... 10 bucks for a roll

When you're tired of people standing too close to you

THIS JUST IN
GRINDS MY GEARS
THE WORLD IS ALMOST OUT OF COMMON SENSE

IF WE COULD JUST GO AHEAD AND START CALLING CHINESE CORONAVIRUS THE KUNG FLU,

THAT WOULD BE GREAT.

#COVID-19

This is a drawing from a kid to remind everyone to wash their hands.

Anyone else who think otherwise go and stand at that corner.

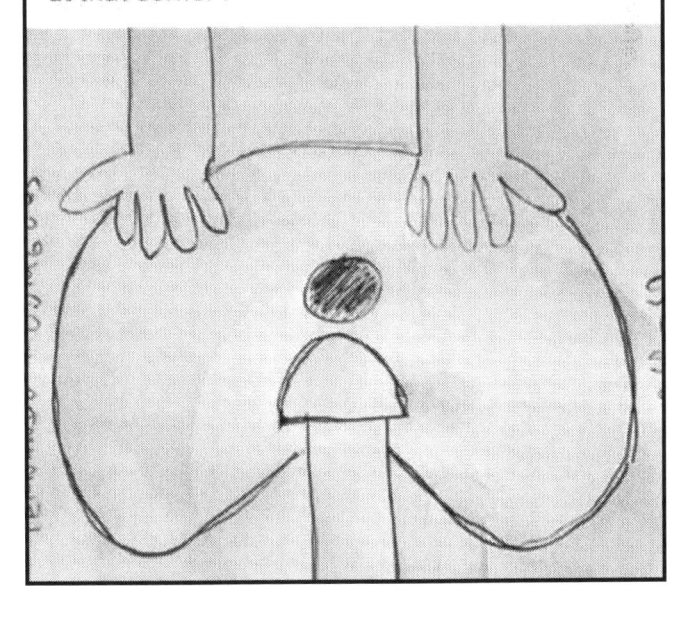

> **HOW ARE WE SUPPOSED TO SAMPLE THIS?**
>
> **WHY IS SHE WEARING GLOVES?**

Kris Kross was right. This shit really is wiggity wiggity whack

It's flu season... If you so much as hiccup near me... I will mace you with Lysol.

when someone hugs you

Panel 1: Sit!!

Panel 3: Damn mask..

Me seeing hand soap shelves empty in stores, wondering why people haven't been washing their hands until now

When a little kid takes a drink out of your water bottle.

In Germany they are preparing for the crisis by stocking up with sausage and cheese.
That's the Wurst Käse scenario.

I HAVE GOT TO STOP SAYING "HOW STUPID CAN YOU BE?"

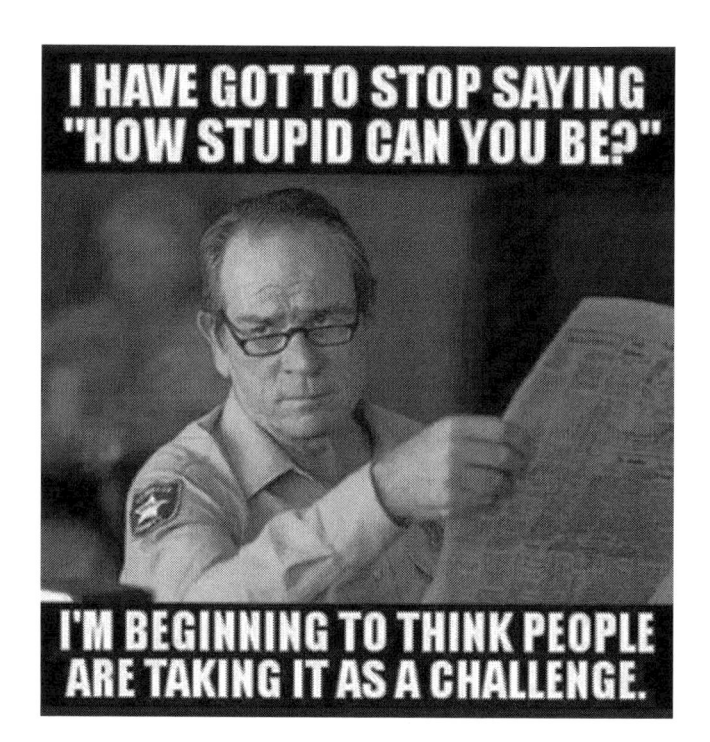

I'M BEGINNING TO THINK PEOPLE ARE TAKING IT AS A CHALLENGE.

And the winner is....

IN WUHAN THIS MEANS YOUR DINNER IS READY

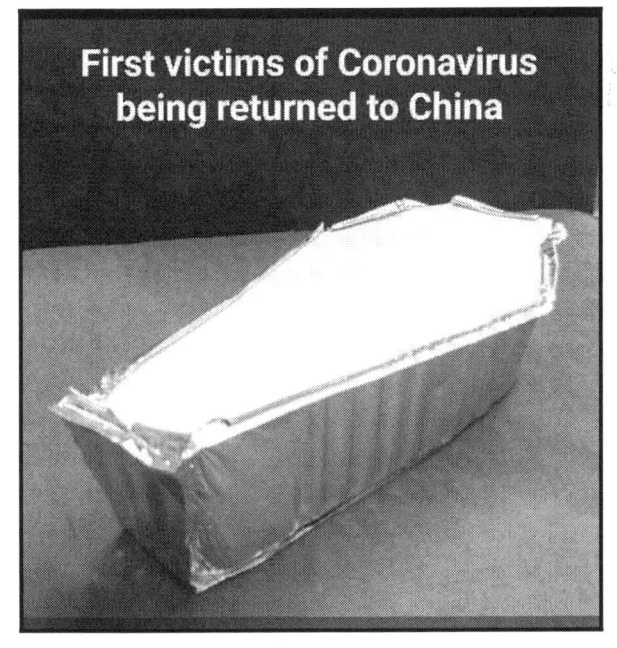

First victims of Coronavirus being returned to China

In the before times, we had daycare, and playgrounds and these places called "restaurants"...
Steve, it's been a week.
nomikane

I'm no expert but Kleenex may want to rethink their box design

Snoopy, I'm afraid of Corona!

Then have a Budweiser!

I USED TO SPIN THAT TOILET PAPER ROLL LIKE I WAS ON THE WHEEL OF FORTUNE

NOW I TURN IT LIKE I'M CRACKING A SAFE

How to give suppository using good social distancing method

Head-nurse Kratchit demonstrates the latest technique in touchless suppository administration.

HOLY 2020 BATMAN, WHAT'S THAT?

IT'S SEEMS TO BE A GIANT TURD, HEADING FOR THAT FAN.

My face mask hides my resting bitch face and unfortunately now people think I'm approachable.

don't touch me, peasant.

You don't actually wash your hands. They wash each other while you stand there looking at them like some kinda creep.

If this picture doesn't sum up our fucking country right now.

We usually shop in the comfort of our own home but the bloody computer crashed

whyatt.com.au

Meanwhile, Inside the fridge

Nicola Sturgeon states that sunbathing is not allowed in Scotland during the lockdown. In response Saudi Arabia has banned skiing.

ME CHECKING OUTSIDE TO MAKE SURE I STILL HATE THE GENERAL PUBLIC

Meanwhile, Inside the fridge

HOW MY FACEBOOK FEED LOOKS RIGHT NOW

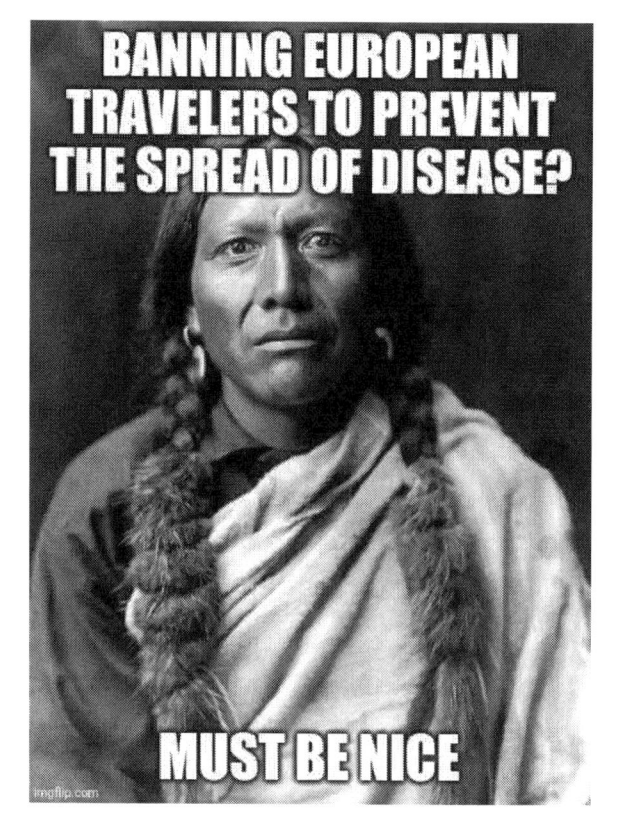

"Put on your masks."

"Kiss our ass!"

BANNING EUROPEAN TRAVELERS TO PREVENT THE SPREAD OF DISEASE?

MUST BE NICE

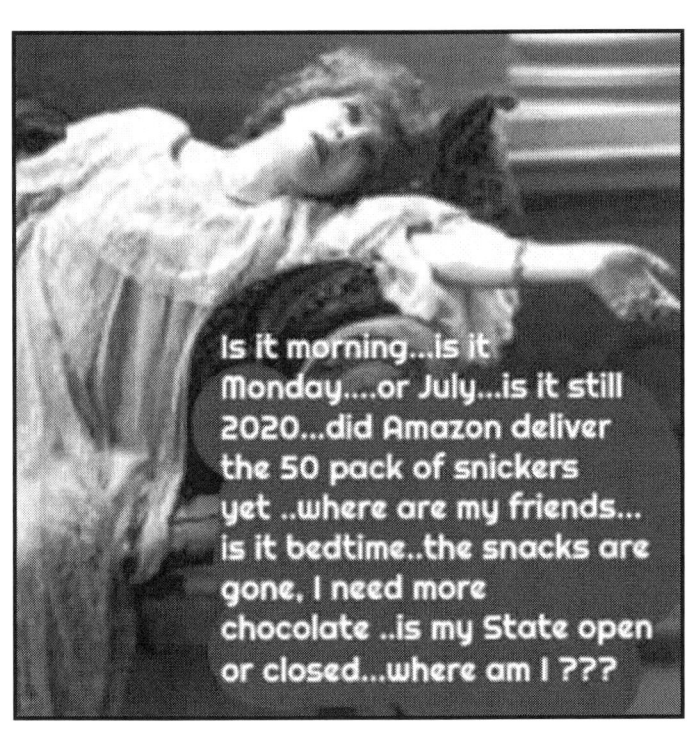

Walmart requiring masks but ass coverings not so much 🤢🤮

Is it morning...is it Monday....or July...is it still 2020...did Amazon deliver the 50 pack of snickers yet ..where are my friends... is it bedtime..the snacks are gone, I need more chocolate ..is my State open or closed...where am I ???

Fuck racism, fuck animal abusers, fuck corona, and fuck coleslaw.

THAT MOMENT YOU GIVE UP LOOKING FOR TOILET ROLLS

WALK AWAY I HAVE ANGER ISSUES and a serious dislike for **STUPID PEOPLE**

It appears we have some breaking news

Good Lord what the fuck now?

At this point, Jesus doesn't need to take the wheel. He needs to pull over & whip some of y'all with his flip flop.

I CAN'T MAKE THIS SHIT UP!

Anil Dash ✓
@anildash

I don't want to be presumptuous, but you can also just wash your hands even if there's *not* some pandemic currently capturing your attention. It doesn't have to be a special occasion.

6:47 AM · 2/29/20 · Twitter for iPhone

If you have survived getting out of one of these drunk you will survive the Corona Virus

Me: *yelling through the front door* THANKS FOR THE DELIVERY. JUST LEAVE THE GROCERIES ON THE DOORSTEP.
Husband: LET ME IN THE FUCKING HOUSE!

BREAKING NEWS

OH WHAT THE FUCK NOW?

IF THE PAST FEW WEEKS HAS TAUGHT US ANYTHING

IT'S THAT STUPIDITY SPREADS FASTER THAN ANY VIRUS EVER COULD

Where is Morgan Freeman? Shouldn't he be narrating this shit or something?

KEEP WATCHING THE NEWS AND THIS IS HOW YOU GONE BE LOOK'N A WEEK FROM NOW

People who drank from the water hose as a kid are immune to Coronavirus.

—Facebook Medical

I'm excited that the phrase "get the fuck away from me" is no longer rude but a public service announcement.
#alwaysanupside

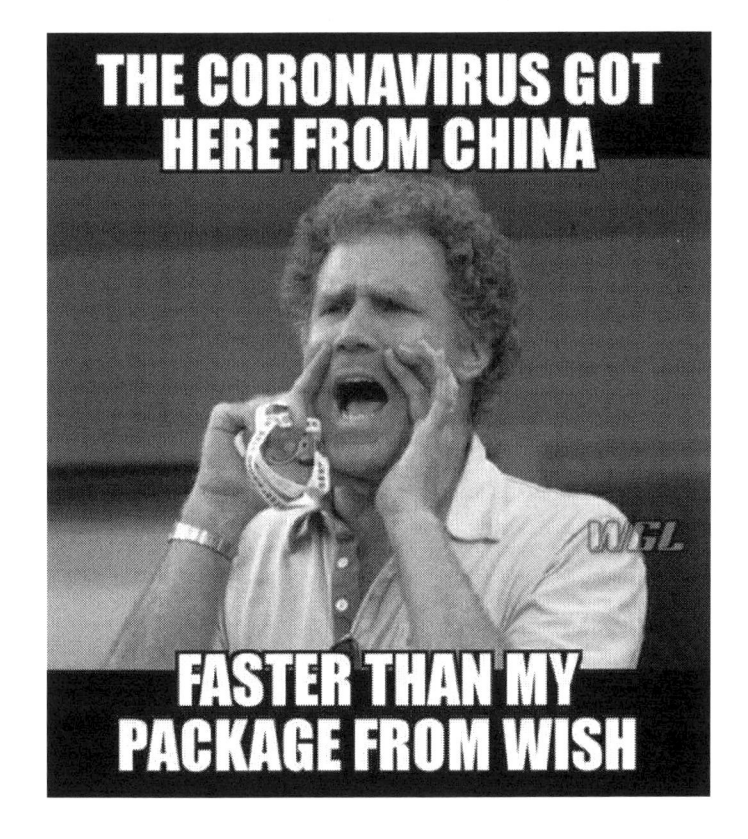

THE CORONAVIRUS GOT HERE FROM CHINA

FASTER THAN MY PACKAGE FROM WISH

Family devastated when pet chews up life savings

Me trying to figure out how "wash your hands" translates to "buy alllll the toilet paper".

Fuck Off! I'm Social Distancing

I'm at a place in my life where errands are starting to count as going out.

It's like we all complained about what a shit year 2019 was and 2020 is like, "here... hold my corona."

SOME PEOPLE AREN'T SHAKING HANDS BECAUSE OF THE CORONAVIRUS,

I'M NOT SHAKING HANDS BECAUSE EVERYONE IS OUT OF TOILET PAPER.

Just back from our cruise. Had a great time.

REMEMBER WHEN WE USED TO ARGUE ABOUT WHICH WAY TO HANG THE TOILET PAPER?

THOSE WERE THE DAYS...

GET OUT OF MY WAY !
Memes 2 by Andy
THE HORNETS ARE COMING !

MURDER HORNETS??
YOU MEAN BASKIN BEES?

GET INSIDE YOUR HOUSE
NO!
RELEASE THE MURDER HORNETS!
THE WHAT...?

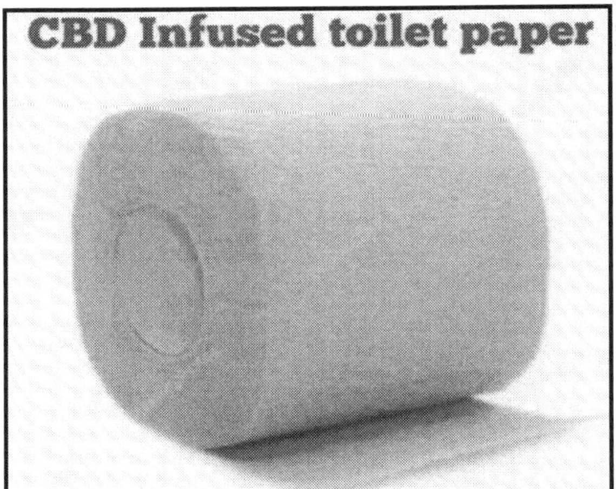
CBD Infused toilet paper
To calm your ass down

LOCKDOWN LIFE

Realizing you can eat peanut butter, out of the jar, naked in the kitchen, without judgment.

Commerative jewellery to always remember 2020.

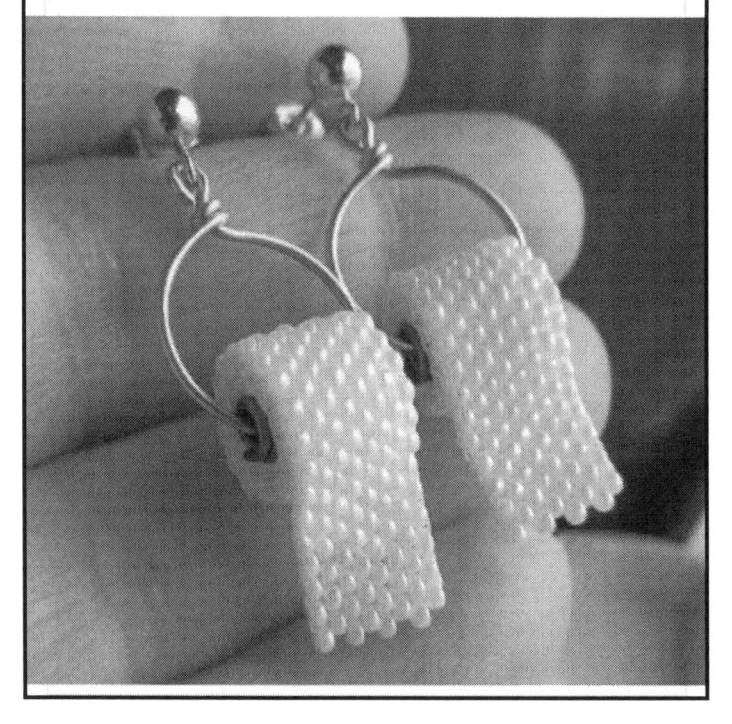

REMEMBER WHEN WE USED TO ARGUE ABOUT WHICH WAY TO HANG THE TOILET PAPER?

THOSE WERE THE DAYS...

"WHY ARE PEOPLE PANIC BUYING," ASKED PIGLET.

"BECAUSE THEY'RE WANKERS," SAID POOH.

Gotta wipe somehow!

All things bright and beautiful.
All creatures great and small.
All things wise and wonderful.
The Chinese eat them all.

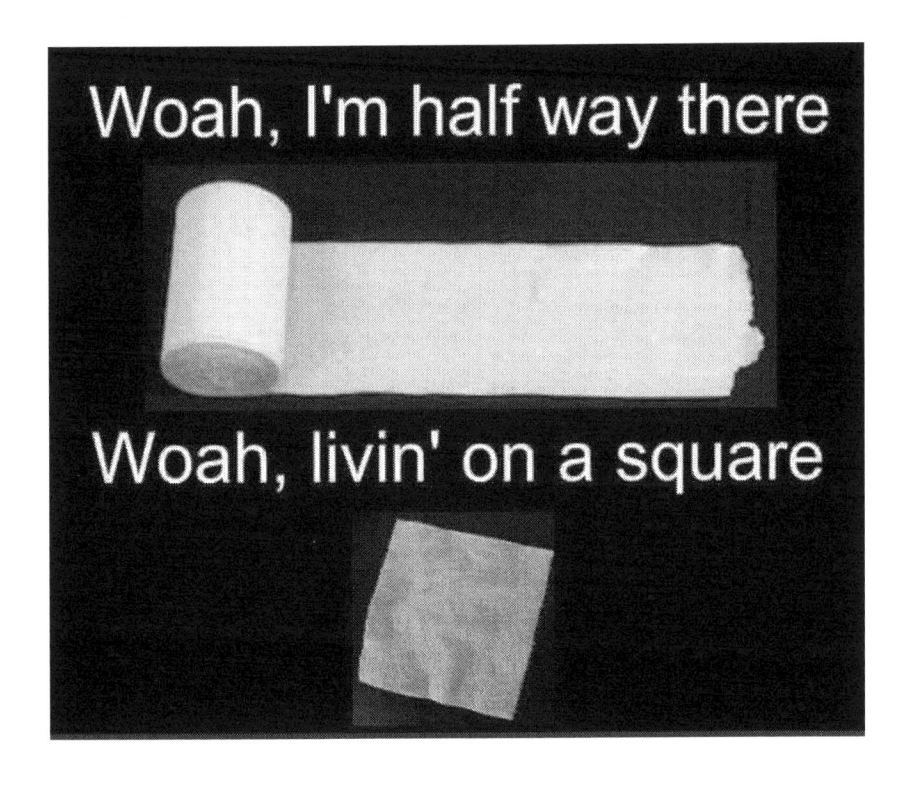

Woah, I'm half way there

Woah, livin' on a square

FINALLY FINISHED MY PANIC ROOM

So I have just been into Walmart..

Honestly it was shocking - they had no toilet paper at all.

Reluctantly I headed for the customer service and asked if they Had any.

A firm NO and a look in disgust was the answer.

Walking back to the toilets with my pants around my ankles was a walk I never want to do again.

WANT ADVANCE NOTICE OF

BOOK 2 CORONAVIRUS

AND OTHER THEMED MEME BOOKS

including

WILDLY OFFENSIVE MEMES

(not for the feint-hearted!)

[CLICK HERE](#)

or email

Mikey [at] wildlyinappropriate.co.uk

Manufactured by Amazon.ca
Bolton, ON